THE 12 BIGGEST BREAKTHROUGHS IN
TRANSPORTATION TECHNOLOGY

by M. M. Eboch

www.12StoryLibrary.com

Copyright © 2015 by Peterson Publishing Company, North Mankato, MN 56003. All rights reserved. No part of this book may be reproduced or utilized in any form or by any means without written permission from the publisher.

12-Story Library is an imprint of Peterson Publishing Company and Press Room Editions.

Produced for 12-Story Library by Red Line Editorial

Photographs ©: Captain Yeo/Shutterstock Images, cover; Tim Roberts Photography/Shutterstock Images, 4; Woe/Shutterstock Images, 5; canebisca/Shutterstock Images, 6; Dragoness/Shutterstock Images, 7; Remy Musser/Shutterstock Images, 8; Library of Congress, 9, 22, 28; A.P. Yates/Library of Congress, 10; Carol M. Highsmith/Library of Congress, 11, 17; Detroit Publishing Co./Library of Congress, 12, 13; Carlos Caetano/Library of Congress, 14; A.G. Renstrom/Library of Congress, 15; Mikhail Kolesnikov/Shutterstock Images, 16, 29; Richard Thornton/Shutterstock Images, 18; Caufield & Shook/Shutterstock Images, 19; jennyt/Shutterstock Images, 20; John T. Daniels/AP Images, 21; Philip Pilosian/AP Images, 23; Artens/Shutterstock Images, 24; Stefan Ataman/Shutterstock Images, 25; Michael Collins/NASA, 26; NASA, 27

ISBN
978-1-63235-017-6 (hardcover)
978-1-63235-077-0 (paperback)
978-1-62143-058-2 (hosted ebook)

Library of Congress Control Number: 2014937355

Printed in the United States of America
Mankato, MN
June, 2014

Go beyond the book. Get free, up-to-date content on this topic at 12StoryLibrary.com.

TABLE OF CONTENTS

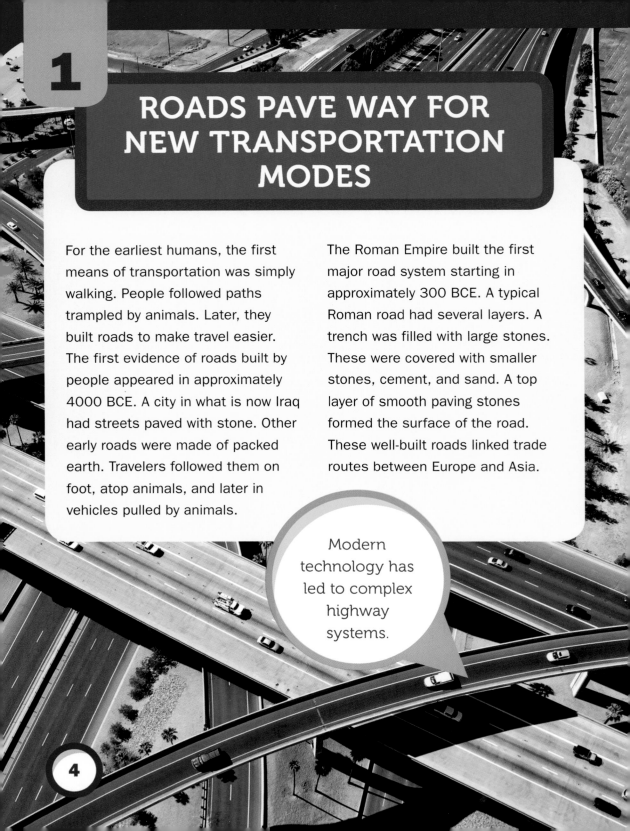

ROADS PAVE WAY FOR NEW TRANSPORTATION MODES

For the earliest humans, the first means of transportation was simply walking. People followed paths trampled by animals. Later, they built roads to make travel easier. The first evidence of roads built by people appeared in approximately 4000 BCE. A city in what is now Iraq had streets paved with stone. Other early roads were made of packed earth. Travelers followed them on foot, atop animals, and later in vehicles pulled by animals.

The Roman Empire built the first major road system starting in approximately 300 BCE. A typical Roman road had several layers. A trench was filled with large stones. These were covered with smaller stones, cement, and sand. A top layer of smooth paving stones formed the surface of the road. These well-built roads linked trade routes between Europe and Asia.

Modern technology has led to complex highway systems.

Rome, Italy, still uses some of its ancient cobblestone roads.

Roads let people travel long distances more quickly and easily. They could move to new places to find food or work. They could trade goods between cities. People also learned about distant places from travelers. Roads connected these places and created the foundation for later forms of transportation.

46,000

Approximate miles (74,030 km) of highways in the US interstate system.

- First used in approximately 4000 BCE in Iraq.
- Made of stones and packed earth and later pavement.
- Helped people travel greater distances.

ROADS ACROSS AMERICA

The first highway to cross the United States was finished in the 1920s. The Lincoln Highway went from New York City to San Francisco, California. In 1956, President Dwight Eisenhower signed the Federal Aid Highway Act. It funded more than 40,000 miles (64,374 km) of roads. In time, highways linked all major cities.

WHEELS LEAD TO FASTER, EASIER TRAVEL

Soon after building the first roads, people invented a better way to travel on them. Ancient pictures show that the wheel was used as early as 3500 BCE in the Middle East. Wooden disks were attached to carts. People or animals pulled the carts to carry loads.

The first wheels were cut from wooden slabs. In approximately 2000 BCE, people started to make wheels with spokes. The spokes connected the center of the wheel with the rim. Spoked wheels were lighter and stronger. They could be used to make lightweight, horse-drawn chariots. At first, wheels used four spokes, then six or eight. Wheels with more spokes were more stable and made for a smoother

Spoked wooden wheels have been used for more than 4,000 years.

An ancient carving shows a chariot pulled by horses.

ride. An axle let the wheels rotate around a central pole. Metal rims reduced wear on the wheel. These advancements were used on wagons and chariots in the Middle East and Europe.

6
Number of spokes in the wheel of an Egyptian war chariot.

- Used as early as 3500 BCE in the Middle East.
- Provided faster transportation.
- Made it easier to transport large loads.
- Used on military chariots.

EGYPTIAN CHARIOTS

Soon after the invention of the wheel, armies started building chariots. A chariot is a two-wheeled carriage that is usually pulled by horses. The Egyptians made lighter, stronger chariots with well-designed harnesses. The chariots could be used to pursue enemies. The chariots gave the Egyptians a military advantage as they expanded their empire beginning in approximately 1550 BCE.

SAILBOATS CATCH WIND FOR EASIER WATER TRAVEL

The earliest humans built boats from logs, reeds, or pieces of bamboo. They tied these materials together to make rafts. By approximately 10,000 BCE, people had improved rafts by pulling animal skins over the frame. Some people made canoes dug out of a single log. They rowed, pushed with poles, or simply let the canoes drift.

The Egyptians developed sailboats in approximately 3200 BCE for travel on the Nile River. Boats could travel downstream by drifting. But sailing helped them travel upstream. Egyptians attached cloth to a mast to catch the wind. It blew into the sail, pushing the boat in the direction the wind was blowing. Most major Egyptian cities were along the Nile, so sailing was an easy means of travel.

Modern sailboats are used for both travel and recreation.

733,000
Number of sailboats in the United States as of 2011.

- First used in 3200 BCE in Egypt.
- Ocean travel possible by 1500 BCE.
- Made coastal cities important.
- Encouraged long-distance trade.

Sailboats have been traveling on the Nile River for thousands of years.

Early ships also used oars to propel the boat when the wind wasn't blowing in the right direction. Over time, sailors figured out how to adjust the sails to move the boat in different directions than the wind was blowing. By 1500 BCE, Egyptian sailboats were sailing the ocean.

Port cities started to spring up along coasts, and more trade occurred between distant lands.

FINDING THE WAY

When covering long distances, travelers need to navigate. The earliest known maps were made on clay tablets from approximately 2300 BCE. The compass also helped. A compass uses a magnet in the shape of a needle. Because of Earth's magnetic field, the needle will always point north. The first compass was used in China in approximately 300 BCE.

STEAM ENGINES POWER TRAINS

The first trains had several carts connected to each other. They were pulled by animals or people along a wooden track. Trains became bigger and faster after the invention of the steam engine in the 1800s. They could carry far more goods for much greater distances.

A steam engine burns coal or wood to heat water. The steam from the water then moves parts in an engine. Several people helped develop steam power and steam trains. Thomas Savery invented a working steam engine in 1698. However, it used a lot of fuel and didn't provide much power.

In 1893, the Empire State Express train was clocked at a speed of 112.5 miles per hour (181 km/h), a record at the time.

85,000

Approximate number of train stations in the United States by 1916.

- Introduced by Matthew Murray in 1804 in England.
- Used steam engine technology developed by James Watt.
- Connected farmland to city markets.
- Became major transportation system for people and goods.

James Watt made a much more efficient steam engine in 1765. It could power moving vehicles of all types.

Matthew Murray of England built the first full-size train engine in 1804. His steam-powered train ran on timber rails. Soon, railroad companies laid tracks across Great Britain and the United States. They linked farmland and cities. The first track to cross from the East to the West Coast of the United States was finished in 1869. Trains became the main mover of people and goods.

This historic steam train at the Grand Canyon Railway uses waste vegetable oil as fuel.

STEAMBOATS RELY LESS ON WIND

Steam technology had a major impact on shipping. Sails only work if there is wind. Steam power solved this problem. In 1806, American Robert Fulton built a new type of boat. His design had a steam engine, a flat bottom, and paddlewheels along the sides. Skeptics called the boat "Fulton's Folly." But it sailed successfully in 1807. Within a few years, steamboats were being used to carry freight on large rivers, such as the Mississippi. Over the next several decades, steamboats became faster. A trip that took 25 days in 1816 took only 4.5 days in 1853.

A steamship docks in Savannah, Georgia, circa 1900.

150

Miles (241 km) traveled by Robert Fulton in his first steamboat voyage on August 7, 1807.

- Introduced by Robert Fulton in 1807 in New York.
- Less dependent on winds.
- Easier to maneuver.
- Increased demand for coal.

A steamboat captain named Moses Rogers helped design the first steamship. Unlike a steamboat, the steamship was designed to cross the ocean. Steamships also replaced earlier warships, which were difficult to steer. By the time of the Civil War (1861–1865), warships used steam power. They still had sails for traveling long distances but used steam engines to maneuver during battle.

TRAVEL TAKES TO THE SKIES WITH HOT AIR BALLOONS

People have been traveling across ground and water routes for thousands of years. But traveling through the air was little more than a dream for most of history. Human flight became a reality in 1783 in France. That was when two brothers, Joseph-Michel and Jacques-Étienne Montgolfier, designed the first hot air balloons.

Before sending people up in a balloon, the brothers wanted to know how high altitude would affect living things. They sent up a balloon with a duck, a rooster, and a sheep on board. The animal passengers landed safely, unharmed. A few months later, a scientist went up in a hot air balloon that was anchored to the ground. Then two people flew in an untied balloon. They traveled more

than five miles (8 km) and landed safely 20 minutes later. This was the first time people experienced flying.

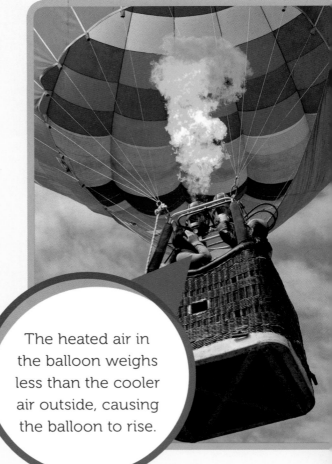

The heated air in the balloon weighs less than the cooler air outside, causing the balloon to rise.

A crowd gathered in Lyon, France, in 1784 to watch one of the first hot air balloons take flight.

25

Miles (40 km) flown in the first hydrogen balloon flight.

- Introduced by Joseph-Michel and Jacques-Étienne Montgolfier in 1783 in France.
- First form of air travel.
- Use hot air or hydrogen.

The first balloons were made of paper and silk. Burning straw heated the air and caused the balloon to rise. But these balloons could catch on fire easily. A few months after the Montgolfiers first flew their balloon, a French inventor flew a balloon that was filled with hydrogen. Balloons that used gas rather than hot air did not require fire. They also could fly farther. Later balloons used a combination of hydrogen and hot air. Balloon travel was expensive and available to few people. But the breakthrough led inventors to search for new and better ways of flying.

AIRSHIPS

Balloons could only drift with the wind. A change in shape, to a long tube, made the balloon easier to steer. Adding an engine gave it more power. In the early 1900s, these airships, or blimps, were used for travel. They did not gain great popularity before being replaced by airplanes. However, some blimps are still in use today.

CABLE CARS AT FOREFRONT OF PUBLIC TRANSPORTATION

Public transportation moves people around cities efficiently and cheaply. Many people can travel together in one vehicle. The earliest versions were streetcars drawn by horses. But inventor Andrew Hallidie noticed how much trouble the horses were having pulling the streetcars up San Francisco's steep hills. He came up with a better way.

Hallidie's father had invented a strong cable that was used in mining. Hallidie used the cable to pull streetcars along a track. The system was powered by a steam engine. Cable cars were first used in San Francisco in 1873. They worked well on the city's steep hills. Soon, the idea spread to other cities.

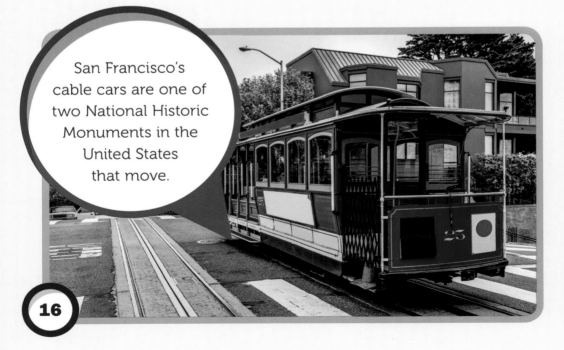

San Francisco's cable cars are one of two National Historic Monuments in the United States that move.

When cable cars need to turn around, they rotate on giant turntables.

San Francisco's cable cars are still used today. But the city uses many other forms of public transportation, too. Electric streetcars and city buses replaced some of the cable cars in the early 1900s. Like other cities, San Francisco started to use trains for public transportation. Trains could travel underground, on the ground, or on raised rails.

19,000

Approximate number of people who rode San Francisco cable cars each day in 2013.

- Invented by Andrew Hallidie in 1873 in San Francisco.
- One of the first public transportation systems.
- Could move large groups of people efficiently.
- Worked well in cities with steep hills.

THINK ABOUT IT

What kinds of public transportation are available where you live? What are some reasons for people to use public transportation?

MODEL T LEADS TO WIDESPREAD CAR OWNERSHIP

The first company to sell cars started in France in 1890. When automobiles first became available to the public, they were very expensive. Few people could afford them. In 1900, approximately 8,000 cars were registered in the United States.

Henry Ford of the Ford Motor Company changed that. In 1908, he introduced the Model T. This car was affordable and dependable. It had a simple gasoline engine and could travel at speeds up to 45 miles per hour (72 km/h). Early models were started by turning a

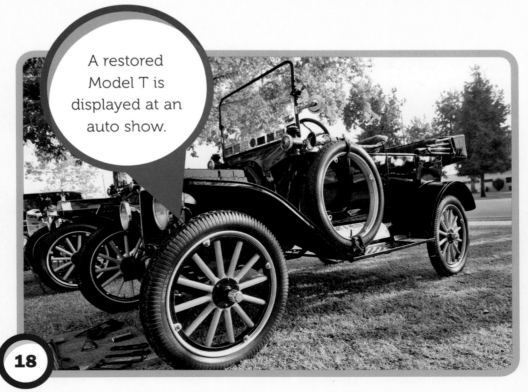

A restored Model T is displayed at an auto show.

Rows of Ford Model T cars await delivery in 1925.

hand crank. After 1920, the Model T had a battery-powered starter. But Ford's major breakthrough was in the factory. He improved machinery to be able to produce parts quickly. Ford also introduced the assembly line. The process of building a car was broken into steps. Each factory worker completed one of the steps. Ford factories started producing cars at a record-breaking rate.

Ford sold almost 15 million Model T cars in the next two decades. Other companies followed his lead and built more affordable cars.

250 million
Number of cars and trucks in the United States in 2014.

- Introduced in 1908 by Ford Motor Company.
- Made possible by the assembly line.
- Low price led to increased car ownership.

HIGHWAYS

Before the Model T, most roads were made of packed dirt. With more cars in use, the government used tax money to build better roads. Eventually thousands of miles of paved roads crossed the country. People no longer needed to live near public transportation. Suburbs grew, and people commuted to work by car.

19

WRIGHT BROTHERS FLY FIRST AIRPLANE

Gliders provided the inspiration for modern flight. A glider is an aircraft that has wings but no engine. Orville and Wilbur Wright became interested in flight after reading about a glider that crashed in 1896. They knew they would need a better way to control the aircraft once it was in the air.

For several years, the Wright brothers experimented with kites and gliders. They tested different wing designs until they figured out what worked. Finally, they built an airplane in 1903. It was powered by a gasoline engine. The first flight attempt crashed after only a few seconds. On the brothers' next

The Wright Brothers Memorial in North Carolina includes a full-size model of the airplane used in the first flight.

120

Distance in feet (36.6 m) traveled by the Wright brothers' first successful flight in 1903.

- Invented by Wilbur and Orville Wright.
- First flight in 1903 in Kitty Hawk, North Carolina.
- Featured improved wing design, gasoline engine.

attempt, the airplane stayed in the air for 12 seconds. The final and longest flight of the day stayed in the air for 59 seconds. It traveled 852 feet (260 m).

The brothers built and tested two more aircraft in 1904 and 1905. Each improved on their previous designs. They flew their third aircraft on October 5, 1905. Wilbur Wright flew 24.5 miles (39.4 km). The flight lasted almost one hour. This proved that the brothers could build an airplane that would remain in the air for a significant amount of time. By 1908, the Wrights had a patent and a contract to sell airplanes to the US Army. Airplanes became important to the military. They were used extensively in World War I (1914–1918). Later, planes were used for transporting cargo and passengers.

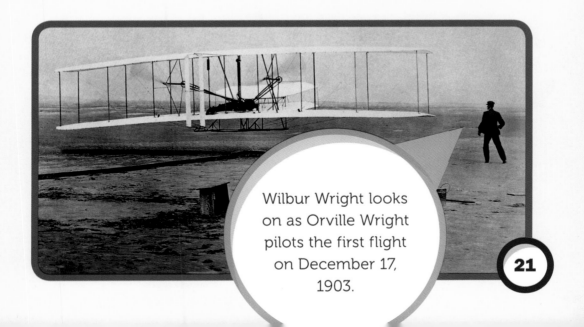

Wilbur Wright looks on as Orville Wright pilots the first flight on December 17, 1903.

JET AIRPLANES FLY FASTER AND FARTHER

In the 1920s, a young pilot in the British Royal Air Force had an idea. Frank Whittle thought that airplanes would be able to fly faster and farther if they could reach higher altitudes. Up high, there is less air resistance. But the engines being used at the time couldn't fly that high. He would have to invent a better engine to test his theory.

Whittle worked on the jet engine for many years. A jet engine burns fuel to produce a stream of hot air and gases. The stream shoots out the back of the engine, pushing it forward. More powerful engines can push airplanes to higher altitudes. In 1941, Whittle's engine was ready to be tested. After a successful test flight, several countries took interest

The Bell XP-59A Airacomet, built in 1942, was the first US jet aircraft.

5,000

Number of jet airplanes in the air over North America at any given time.

- Developed by Frank Whittle, 1920s–1930s.
- Made long-distance air travel possible.
- Increased tourism.
- Provided faster transportation of goods.

in the technology. US companies started building jet aircraft in 1942.

Great Britain used jet aircraft beginning in 1944. These planes could go more than 500 miles per hour (805 km/h). The following years brought more powerful engines. Modern jet airplanes can travel more than 1,000 miles per hour (1,609 km/h).

With the new technology, air travel became a popular mode of long-distance travel. People could go across the country or around the world. More people were able to visit foreign countries. Mail and goods could also travel quickly by jet airplane.

Passenger jets fly at altitudes up to 39,000 feet (11,887 m).

ELECTRIC MOTORS REDUCE DEPENDENCY ON GAS

When people first built cars, they experimented with several types of engines. Some cars used steam or electrical power. By the 1920s, these were rejected. Gasoline engines proved more efficient and reliable. But gasoline engines cause pollution, and fuel is expensive. Looking for other options, inventors decided to give electric cars another try.

Some countries in Europe have started offering public electric cars, available to rent for short trips. They can be picked up at charging stations on certain roads.

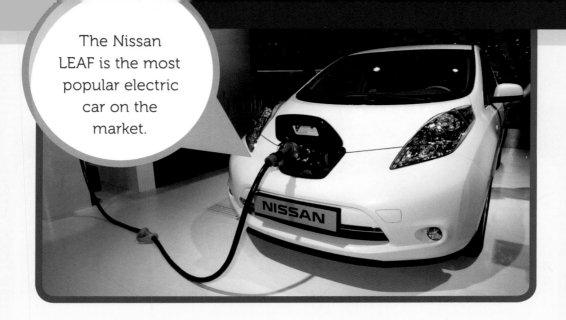

The Nissan LEAF is the most popular electric car on the market.

The first fully electric vehicle came out in 1974. Bob Beaumont invented the CitiCar. He was inspired by the battery-powered moon rover. The CitiCar had a top speed of approximately 30 miles per hour (48 km/h). It could only go 40 miles (64 km) before needing a charge. It was sold for only a few years.

Later attempts combined an electric motor with a gasoline engine. These vehicles are called hybrids. Hybrids use the electric motor at low speeds and the gasoline engine at higher speeds. The gas engine also charges the electric motor. Thousands of hybrid cars have been sold. In the meantime, scientists have continued to work on better models that use just electricity. The 2013 Nissan LEAF can travel up to 90 miles (145 km) on one charge. It can be used for short trips, such as commuting to work.

50

Miles per gallon (21 km/L) of a 2014 Toyota Prius, making it the most fuel-efficient midsize hybrid on the market.

- Introduced by Bob Beaumont in 1974.
- Used in hybrid cars along with gasoline engines.
- Used in fully electric cars that can travel short distances.

SPACE RACE SENDS ASTRONAUTS TO THE MOON

In 1957, the Soviet Union launched a satellite into Earth's orbit. The satellite, called Sputnik 1, was approximately the size of a beach ball. It launched the space race between the Soviet Union and the United States. The two countries spent the 1960s developing ways to send astronauts into space.

In 1961, the United States announced the Apollo space program. The project's goal was to land on the moon. Each Apollo spacecraft was attached to a launch vehicle, called Saturn V. Powerful rocket engines on Saturn V launched the spacecraft into space. Once it reached the moon, the spacecraft

Apollo 11's lunar module orbits the moon before taking the astronauts down to the surface.

Apollo 11 launches on July 16, 1969, from Kennedy National Space Center.

went into orbit. A lunar module detached to take the astronauts down to the moon's surface. Apollo spacecraft successfully reached the moon six times. Apollo 11 became the first to land successfully in 1969. Americans Buzz Aldrin and Neil Armstrong were the first people to walk on the moon.

Sending people into space and safely bringing them back was a major feat. But unmanned space travel has been important for discovery, too. Unmanned spacecraft have taken pictures and gathered samples from the moon. They have explored Mars and produced close-up photos of other planets.

543

Number of people who have been in space as of March 2014.

- Apollo space program started in 1961.
- 33 Apollo flights, 11 of which were manned.
- Apollo 11 landed on the moon on July 20, 1969.

THINK ABOUT IT

Do you think space travel is important? What do you think scientists can learn by exploring space?

FACT SHEET

- During the 1920s and 1930s, several daring pilots set flight records or made history in other ways. Charles Lindbergh flew from New York City to Paris, France, in 1927. His trip took 33.5 hours. Richard Byrd was the first pilot to fly over the North Pole in 1926. He made the first flight over the South Pole in 1929. In 1931, Wiley Post flew around the world in eight days. The following year, Amelia Earhart became the first female pilot to fly across the Atlantic Ocean. These accomplishments showed people how much airplane technology was improving.

- Before air travel was possible, people could only cross large bodies of water by boat. It took two months to get from Europe to New York City in a sailboat. A large modern ship with an engine can make the trip in approximately one week. An airplane can make the flight in less than eight hours.

- The National Aeronautics and Space Administration (NASA) is the US government agency for space exploration. It was founded in 1958.

- Many forms of transportation release greenhouse gases into the air. Greenhouse gases include carbon dioxide, methane, and other chemicals that are released into the air when fuel is burned. Transportation accounts for more than 25 percent of greenhouse gases being released into the atmosphere in the United States.

- Most modern trains are no faster than those in the 1890s. This could change with Magnetic Levitation trains. These MAGLEV trains use powerful magnets. The magnetic field allows the train to levitate. There is no contact between the train and the rails. This lets the train travel much faster. It also causes less wear on the tracks.

- The first high-speed passenger train was completed in Japan in 1964. At first, it could travel up to speeds of 130 miles per hour (210 km/h). Many other countries have added high-speed trains since then. Modern high-speed rail lines can reach speeds of up to 221 miles per hour (356 km/h).

GLOSSARY

air resistance
The force of air pushing against a moving object, also called drag.

altitude
The height of something, such as an airplane, above sea level.

commute
To travel some distance to and from work on a regular basis.

efficient
Using less energy or resources.

engine
A machine with moving parts that converts energy into motion.

goods
Products that are bought for use.

navigate
To direct the course of a ship, aircraft, or other mode of transportation.

patent
Approval from a government to an inventor that says others cannot make, use, or sell that invention without permission.

satellite
An object in orbit around a planet or a moon.

spokes
The bars or rods that connect the center of a wheel to the outer edge.

suburb
An area where people live that is near to but outside the main part of a city.

vehicle
A machine used to transport people or objects.

FOR MORE INFORMATION

Books

Buckley, James, Jr. *Who Were the Wright Brothers?* New York: Grosset & Dunlap, 2014.

Floca, Brian. *Locomotive*. New York: Atheneum Books for Young Readers, 2013.

Lassieur, Allison. *The Race to the Moon: An Interactive History Adventure*. North Mankato, MN: Capstone, 2014.

Spengler, Kremena T. *An Illustrated Timeline of Transportation*. North Mankato, MN: Nonfiction Picture Books, 2011.

Transportation. New York: DK Children, 2012.

Walker, Robert. T*ransportation Inventions: Moving Our World Forward*. New York: Crabtree, 2013.

Websites

NASA Ultra-Efficient Engine Technology Kid's Page
www.grc.nasa.gov/WWW/k-12/UEET/StudentSite

Smithsonian National Air and Space Museum
airandspace.si.edu

Smithsonian National Museum of American History: America on the Move
amhistory.si.edu/onthemove

INDEX

About the Author

M. M. Eboch writes about science, history, and culture for all ages. Her novels for young people include historical fiction, ghost stories, and action-packed adventures.

READ MORE FROM 12-STORY LIBRARY

Every 12-Story Library book is available in many formats, including Amazon Kindle and Apple iBooks. For more information, visit your device's store or 12StoryLibrary.com.